THE POETRY OF HASSIUM

The Poetry of Hassium

Walter the Educator

Silent King Books

SILENT KING BOOKS

SKB

Copyright © 2024 by Walter the Educator

All rights reserved. No part of this book may be reproduced in any manner whatsoever without written permission except in the case of brief quotations embodied in critical articles and reviews.

First Printing, 2024

Disclaimer
This book is a literary work; poems are not about specific persons, locations, situations, and/or circumstances unless mentioned in a historical context. This book is for entertainment and informational purposes only. The author and publisher offer this information without warranties expressed or implied. No matter the grounds, neither the author nor the publisher will be accountable for any losses, injuries, or other damages caused by the reader's use of this book. The use of this book acknowledges an understanding and acceptance of this disclaimer.

"Earning a degree in chemistry changed my life!"
– Walter the Educator

dedicated to all the chemistry lovers, like myself, across the world

HASSIUM

Hassium stands alone,

HASSIUM

A symbol of scientific endeavor, in discovery it's shown.

HASSIUM

With atomic number 108, it claims its place,

HASSIUM

In the periodic table's intricate embrace.

HASSIUM

Born from fusion, in a lab's controlled domain,

HASSIUM

Synthesized with precision, its existence we attain.

HASSIUM

Named after Hesse, the land where scholars roam,

HASSIUM

Hassium emerges, in laboratories its home.

HASSIUM

A fleeting presence, elusive and shy,

HASSIUM

Its properties mysterious, to scientists' eye.

HASSIUM

Unraveling its secrets, in experiments' dance,

HASSIUM

Revealing its essence, in each fleeting chance.

HASSIUM

In particle accelerators, with energies high,

HASSIUM

Nuclei collide, in a cosmic sky.

HASSIUM

Protons and neutrons, in a cosmic brawl,

HASSIUM

Merge and transform, in a subatomic sprawl.

HASSIUM

Within the chaos, new atoms arise,

HASSIUM

Among them, Hassium, a noble prize.

HASSIUM

But fleeting it is, like a shooting star's gleam,

HASSIUM

Existing briefly, in a subatomic dream.

HASSIUM

Its stability fleeting, its half-life short,

HASSIUM

In microseconds it exists, then it's naught.

HASSIUM

Yet in that brief moment, it leaves its mark,

HASSIUM

A testament to science's eternal spark.

HASSIUM

In the universe vast, where elements roam,

HASSIUM

Hassium's presence whispers, in a silent tome.

HASSIUM

A testament to human curiosity's flight,

HASSIUM

Pushing boundaries, seeking knowledge's light.

HASSIUM

So let us marvel at Hassium's grace,

HASSIUM

In the realm of elements, it finds its place.

HASSIUM

A symbol of discovery, of human endeavor,

HASSIUM

Unraveling mysteries, now and forever.

HASSIUM

In laboratories adorned with scientific might,

HASSIUM

Researchers toil ceaselessly, in the pursuit of light.

HASSIUM

Their instruments precise, their minds alight,

HASSIUM

Seeking Hassium's secrets, hidden from sight.

HASSIUM

Through the veil of uncertainty, they press on,

HASSIUM

Driven by curiosity, until the break of dawn.

HASSIUM

In their quest for knowledge, they stand tall,

HASSIUM

Unlocking the mysteries of Hassium, once and for all.

HASSIUM

ABOUT THE CREATOR

Walter the Educator is one of the pseudonyms for Walter Anderson. Formally educated in Chemistry, Business, and Education, he is an educator, an author, a diverse entrepreneur, and he is the son of a disabled war veteran. "Walter the Educator" shares his time between educating and creating. He holds interests and owns several creative projects that entertain, enlighten, enhance, and educate, hoping to inspire and motivate you.

Follow, find new works, and stay up to date
with Walter the Educator™
at WaltertheEducator.com

www.ingramcontent.com/pod-product-compliance
Lightning Source LLC
LaVergne TN
LVHW051921060526
838201LV00060B/4110